# when new time folds up

# when new time folds up

## Kathleen Fraser

Chax Press

Minneapolis 1993

Parts of this book appear in the magazines *Hambone, 6ix, Abacus, o•blēk,* in the letterpress printed series *Fascicles,* and in the anthology *The Art of Practice.*

The work of art on the cover of this book is a handmade paper painting by Mary Hark, 1993 artist in residence at Minnesota Center for Book Arts, Minneapolis. It is reproduced courtesy of the artist, who retains all rights for further reproduction.

Chax Press
P.O. Box 19178
Minneapolis, Minnesota 55419-9178
612-724-3004
Fax: 612-724-3016

ISBN 0-925904-14-7

Library of Congress Cataloging-in-Publication Data

Fraser, Kathleen, date
    When new time folds up / Kathleen Fraser
        p.  cm.
    ISBN 0-925904-14-7 (paperback : acid-free) : $11.00
    I.  Title
PS3556.R353W53     1993
811'.54--dc20                                                93-35570
                                                               CIP

Chax Press is distributed by
Inland Book Company, P.O. Box 120261, East Haven, CT 06512
Small Press Distribution Inc, 1814 San Pablo, Berkeley, CA 94702

*for Tony Richardson*

# ETRUSCAN PAGES

*Yet the Etruscan blood continued to beat. And Giotto and the early sculptors seemed to have been a flowering again of the Etruscan blood, which is always putting forth a flower and always being trodden down again by some superior force.*

*D.H. Lawrence*

*Prologo*

Norchia, day of error

half a tin sign nailed to wooden post


"*olis*" of *necropolis*   hanging there


Same wrong direction, again, olive groves
running backwards through rented window

"bearded" as in grain's awn, gold oats


blur each side of several white roads

Cumulus arrives and closes over us

grey-headed carrion crow repeats its descent

A traveler, not understanding the bird's motive
notes the beauty of its ruffled, fog-colored hood
as it rises

mulberry *mare, mar Tirreno*
lean spare Tyrrhenian sea

&bull;

Quick finches scale air

In the ravine, a presence

&bull;

Feeling around for something lost . . .

(The soundtrack, now that I think of it, made all the difference
in the film . . . I carried the music in my head for years, what it
located that was not in the world, at least not in a world I knew.)

&bull;

wind sifts iron filings'
carelessly drawn script

downhill writing
carved with metal object

or red and black brushed with finger
into soft stone recess

above the place they lay the dead one

.

we know what each mark is equal to
but not, in retrospect, what was intended

.

wanting messages, "little sentences
freely written in red paint or black"

*Tarquinia*

Wind skidding grey Maremma
wide and water-logged

Walking from the Palazzo's archeological graft

"Nothing, nothing there,"
someone said
of the places we longed for
where the dead lived under us

in their little painted houses
gazing at yellow walls

episodic, chromatic

•

Sheep's cloudy asymmetry

tomb hum
where more than one dancer

lifts a muscular red thigh
or rests

head carved to wide bone enigma
at death
matched by carver
to any stone torso's likeness

inscribed with the hidden
particularity of one still alive

*I am Larthia*

first words

found

You lie there semi-recumbent

with extravagant, elongated
limbs and weight of belly falling
always more away
from us

refusing cold white grief

Greek traders bartering classic marble through flat Tyrrhenian

or you choose a stone lid look-alike

a kind of mirror
that later will cover the urn
in which your body is light and porous
as volcanic ash

your "clumsy lavishness" and heavy mascara

*Urn Pictures*

.     .     .

birds  birds
in a little flight up

he flings his stone
to ruin them
sex erect under rough shirt

boys in boat
let string down
in waves

dolphin dives
duck walks on water

.     .     .

            .     .     .

            amphora bodies' black slant

            in squeeze of light
            two women

            one on her knees

            in front of
            the other standing

            holding the lamp
            to shine on

            her lover's curiosity

            .     .     .

15

   •    •    •

balancing

her, back-to-
back on the second

man who's down on
all fours
like a table top

he gives it to her

unreservedly

   •    •    •

         •    •    •

In the same back room
another "Greek" vase

gone viscous
with birdlime

liminal
(at the back door
of the demon's rump

he thumbs and struggles
struggles and thumbs

         •    •    •

Etruscan women lie languorously
with what they love

roast little pigs for weddings
serve figs

are equal in all divination
(reading livers of sacrificed animals)

Rome sends young men to Etruscan women
for wisdom

In war propaganda
they called her audacious

on her feet and
dancing the blue striped salute

to his blond hair and red painted body
naked with wine jar

She is survived by her fringed scarf
tossed over a tree limb

Rome's greed for metals

melting her down

Dear Annalisa,

I'm replaying this morning's phone call, hearing the stagger of my half-awake mind in Italian (after six hours sleep) as I tried to make some sort of meaning for you out of my trip to Vulci and Norchia . . . imagining your patient face at the other end of the telephone, filling in the blanks . . . but there is yet more to tell you.

We left Thursday morning at seven sharp with maps and a mostly useless little guidebook that only came in handy around two o'clock when we were suddenly hungry and in the middle of "nowhere." We wanted to eat something fresh from the nearby woods and herbaceous fields — A. wanted cinghiale (scene of wild boar crashing through underbrush), S. wanted funghi porcini and country olives, I was thinking of rughetta and tomatoes with a bottle of green olive oil on the table. Our book held out the lure of a farmhouse near Vulci that served roasted game and grilled fish. (What is that smile passing over your face?) After a phone call from the nearest town bar, we went back along the same road, away from the temple site, and passed the overhang of the bridge, looking all the time for some plausible stopping place. The wind was up again and we wanted a fire.

Lawrence wrote that the Etruscans "vanished as completely as flowers" . . . this language asks for alum. We know they built everything from their vast and cultivated forests — wooden houses, wooden ships — except for certain bridges and retaining walls . . . and that they wrote most of their texts on wood, saving important inscriptions for metal plates which were probably melted down and re-used by Gauls threatening from the north or the disciplined, war-minded Romans . . .

(A little story for you)

With his companion, D., and between the great world wars, the writer hustles locals for food (some cheese? a bit of cured beef?) while waiting for the baker's boy and the baker's horse to unhitch from delivering bread. D. returns from the street, suspicious of the small and spotted oranges. But they are "sweet as apples", eaten with sausage and country bread. They wait.

We are close by at the Osteria, eating cinghiale in our pasta.

Your reading of "conjecture" in the Creeley-Olson correspondence stays with me . . .I hope that your essay is coming together.

*A presto, e con affetto,*

K

*Norchia*

A The letter A is a plow
(mare pulling into *ma*re)
   horse plowing sea
   Maremma

      Was A
      where
you made and
      unmade your mind . . .


first hesitation

      when you doubted
   what you
      thought you
      were
   looking for?



.

alpha. aslant. alien. appal. answer. anodic. alum. *A.*

stooping. struggle. squeeze of light. sling. slate. shut. scrutiny. *S.*

ropy. *R.* viscous. *V.* overhang. *O.* hold. hover. *H.* boar. *B.* follow. flush. *F.* herbaceous. *H.*

.

$$\Lambda 2 \wedge \text{I} \Phi \text{R}$$

"we know what each mark is equal to, but in retrospect . . ."

red paint or black

.

another progression of ants across dry mud ruts

this abandoned road mapped with their cultivated huts and paths

they continue in dry weather in wind

deliberate burdens through the temporal

He isn't here, nor his page of exertion
No close-written excavation of particulars

to inscribe a limit
Footstep's parallel replica

such breathing

(still, a pressing flutter climbs with us
down and through stone)

Lava revetments
retain precipitous bluffs —

(ashlars compose a frame for each entering dead one)

lintel of their own Alpha

Tombs carpentered shut
as if made of wood

(scrutiny of stone mason
eyeing his painted house
on ravine's opposite bank)

rooms carved with tools

For the journey
ductile metal
malleable gold fibula
gold spiral for curls


bronze mirror
(stooping, Thetis
curves P. close behind)

. . . a Gr. story
but an Etruscan has scratched
        *Herecele + Mlacuch*

over it
in her own hand

Death imagines us into pleasure. We want to continue

We stand in front of the dark abandoned tunnel
a tomb where all has been emptied and carted
to the villa —

a thick glass door we will open
(the museum keeper's blink)

Leaves are massing, green speeding up

We are not dressed in wide straw hats with grosgrain bands
our make-up is not elaborate

but we want a record of us where there is "nothing"
as if by holding each other's waists, we could
find the border and lose it

No plan for this bargain      Take our picture

14 . June . 1991

Dear Susan,

"An isolated fact, cut loose from the universe, has no significance for the poet. It derives its significance from the reality to which it belongs." (Wallace Stevens, "On Poetic Truth")

The night after you left for Paros, I dreamt I was lying on a stone slab at the base of the cliff tombs at Norchia, preparing to make my transition from "this world" to "the other." I was thinking about how to negotiate the passage, when it came to me — the reason for all the layers of fine white cloth arranged and spread around me. I said to you (because you were with me), "You just keep wrapping yourself with white cloth and eventually you are in the other place."

I wanted to write about the trip but I couldn't find words for those places at once so peaceful and full of what was & wasn't there. Two nights later I dreamt, again, of Norchia. This time Norma had come there to work on engravings. She asked me if I'd work on them with her. I began assembling evidence after that, scratching with my red and black ink down the pages of the new ledger you'd given me . . . all fragmentary . . .

Today—exactly a week since your face went by inside the window of the cab—a classical archeologist phoned up to have a look at our place (he'd seen our rental announcement). He knew Norchia and the cliff tombs and we talked about the mystery surrounding the Etruscan language. "We still have no idea . . . beyond family names and lineage or sometimes an inscription to a particular god or goddess . . . one doesn't have much to go on, with tombs as your main reference." Then he recalled several other sources under study — two plates [rectangles] of fine-beaten gold, covered with text, found in the temples at Pyrgi (very near where we were, but closer to the sea . . . I saw the plates at the Villa Giulia

26

in Rome on Sat. and they are the size of letter pages with nail holes distributed around their edges, as if pounded into a wooden door or wall).

     ———————          ———————

     •  •  •          •  •  •

     •    •          •    •

     •  •  •          •  •  •
     ———————          ———————

The other source is the "mummy wrapping," linen originally from Egypt (probably hauled on trading ships), and covered with formulaic and repetitious Etruscan religious precepts — written "retro" (right to left). Even though there are over 1,500 words covering it, the total lexicon is barely 500. The mummy text is preserved in the museum in Zagreb, YUG., thus "The Zagreb Mummy." When they found her in Etruria, her body had been wrapped in this shroud made of pieces of linen, written on through centuries . . . used as "pages" for new writing whenever the old text had faded. Her family had wrapped her in this cloth, this writing, because it was available.

I have no letter from you yet. Margy's daughter, Ariana, comes tonight for supper with a friend (a little like having M. here) . . . Arthur will make his famed *spaghetti vongole —" per morire"* (to die for)

With dreamed stylus in wakeful hand — and many empty pages — I send you love, imagining you half in, half out of the water.

K

*Vulci*


To shed time   *Fibula sanguisuga:* The pin of gold beadwork
with tiny winged lions (promised in the book)
was not there

We are here   (Fibula fabula, blood fable)


The museum at Vulci (former *badia* for local monks)
grips its rough medieval ramparts

Romans who bought extensively from thieves
(restored urns for their own shelves)
called these patched fragments "Greek"

arrogating evidence
with patient smiles

finding the workmanship skillful
and attributing value to retrieval


*Fibula:* pin; clasp. *The bone in man is a clasp.*

*Sanguisuga:* leech. *The leech in man is a clasp of blood.*

Where was it the malaria began, yellow and slow
malarial hunks of tufo cliffs
cut and joined at indefinite perimeters

On each new edge rests an imagined approximation
cut from cooled lava. Hard, bubbly nothing

"Nothing there," no masonry to support it



Vulci once
kept men in or out

Vulci, route to copper
(flamingos along wet stretches)

where bats hung from tomb roofs and
scattered against the writer's shoulder
when he crawled the passages
which led to nothing

there in the stubby light

*Ponte dell' Abbadia* (Vulci)


Etruscan foundation, Roman arch (severe parabola)

narrow walkway wide enough for territorial smuggle

Ponte dell' Abbadia, a pure transaction
but for mineral pouring from continuous run-off

rains and rains' steady thieving

increasing, belligerent

as if the bridge had formed, half way over
a scar in air

torn piece from eyelid's curve
pulled down

not classical

calling up grief


.


(The soundtrack of that film . . . I feared the music, in retro-
spect . . . as if it were foretelling everything coming toward
me . . . paths moving with choral inevitability towards all I
would love and finally lose . . . my own path calling me.)·

Under it
levels of water

rivers
among them the Fiora rising
a manageable springing gush

asphodel, pinkish & ivory
"sparking"




Randy sea, let in
where mosquitoes bred and doubled

Trees in slow motion fall to
stagnate puddles' original green leaking

Something like shadow, a grey thing
color of carrion, falls

Old warning on metal gate

[*VIPERE*]

Ruts in road partly mud, wild finocchio

You get out to open the gate

imagining *V*

your shoes sink down

The car plows through groundhold of tumuli

temple rubble abandon

anodic slate light

Grief is simple and dark

as this bridge or hidden field
where something did exist once

and may again, or
your face receding behind the window

a possible emptying


.

Make copies, please

of each framed motion
grey sheep heavy, milky

I am needing proof

heather, purple thistle

audacious poppy
late, and everywhere red

Vulci, mouth of iron
and port to minerals, inland

No one passes Vulci or crosses her bridge

(this boundary you make up in your mind)

without vessels, seed, paint, vines
and codex of blue stripe and blue leaves

Mulberry smeared clover
covers an entire field

Invisible beds
where once stagnant shallows bred malarial cells

Before that

dancers

June, 1991
Trastevere (Rome), once called *Litus Etruscus*

# FRAMMENTI ROMANI:

"marks and evidence of events"

— for the photographer, Kenneth Josephson

Ache
drawn border's arousal

    Arise new radio gleeful
    to them

— these loud-struck ochre spaces —
re-heard and re-
sung little
motorscooter vices,

Repeat the fruited song
gone wings, what

    is farthest
    hear

Accede shadow able,

redoubtable cycle,

green when awake now.

Noble hairpin

spring's prong

block-long cyclone

To accelerate

  (radiant outward from her)

radial's own wave

Porcelain light opens

plum waist, wool-sweet cape of

  thunder's borders.

Pulled out and re-drawn

  "the relation of real color"

to soaked walls, a difference of
squash persimmon exteriors

  — Michelangelo, given the choice,
retaliates —

in restauro's reserve
massive wave of Roman brick
and door

Yawn also
single balconey's coral geraniums

In thicket eyes as in
pollened
yellow streams of mimosa
given

(that flower stuck tile

ceramic-struck
field forever, some
nature's ideal),

bellowing leaves,
pared stems seeds skins make

noon's hollow noise.

Now pried from hand's huge fabric clouds

    amorphous
    off-white
    awry

but    could    yet    see

could spot exactly where
to keep the illumined
alum honey hive-
ing

" . . . put honeycomb there with
slabs of gorgonzola
on the bare
table, spread
the walnut bread with it
and a little
honey
and the Barolo from
Aldo Conterno . . ."

(How more
could you be

third-person
bound for scrutiny?

Barolo-dark sea)

Closest,
restored sections of

what is farthest

late drawn borders
re-examined

pulled out as "cuts"

    (resistant
    that tiny sweet "heart" of

oxygen's nerve)

Written in sleep's fore-glow
mid-afternoon
pallor struck light

    Light before dog
    rubber noise
    hose elaborate

street's papaya dense plaster
pessimism
    clarified surface duress

Aware. O here.

Be there, too, savory rattle.

Afternoon's little zipper
pulls you up each fruiting
rutting assault. Leaves contend!
Pips grow larger even. And figs soon.
Bend.

Tight fist that held you,
you entirely separate —

what is mortal
in this body.

Rome
July, 1990

# GIOTTO : ARENA

:

Another I beheld, than blood more red
A goose display of whiter wing than curd.
And one who bore a fat and azure swine
Pictured on his white scrip, addressed me thus:
What doest thou in this deep? Go now and know,
Since yet thou livest, that my neighbor here,
Vitaliano, on my left shall sit.

Dante's *Inferno*, Canto XVii
(trans. Rev. Henry Francis Cary, 1805)

Fat blood
addressed me,
thus this deep
curd.
Now know
thou live more
red than good.
"I did,"
Scrovegno said.

                    living to sit obscured by word "here"

GIOTTO

:

ARENA

:


Enrico, son of Reginaldo
  SCROVEGNO
(money-lender of
peak avaricious habits
confirmed by cameo spot
in Dante's seventh circle),

offers his earnest version of atonement
for paternal embarrassment
and hopes for better treatment, too,
in Padova, bringing all glory
to the Virgin Annunciate


continuing Lady's Day
but doing it right, with Giotto's
brush to introduce him                                of

                                                        avarice
            ARENA                                       effect

new name, old site, chapel built
above more than one original,
the first an amphitheatre cast
along Roman lines

            ARENA

Enrico on his knees proffers
a tiny version of it
to the Annunciate, its weight
supported on another's shoulders,
salmon length of brick the same
as Virgin's gown, angel feathers'


salmon flesh and roe
lifting one swift arc


Enrico Scrovegno of Padova
on this spot defamed


remains of Romans

motion (less leaves) blue sky

                    inlaid their branching
lightness
                    pale rose breadth

of shade
through intervals


Dante watched Giotto paint Enrico
(they talked at Arena)

.

"Not by system, but by
wrist,"
G. said,
substituting body parts.

pale rose
bread

"Odd arch
of nose,

did you notice?"

___massed_____
He masses pale clothed bodies — relieved with beloved and
random Venetian stripes; blue is sparingly ppressedd . . .

## A certain Flemish meanness

Graven image temporarily misplaced . . . the possible
enlargement of a click(ed) moment's pictorial efforts, Giotto
keeps looking at grasses' breadth, a band of green repeated
not in stone but in lines' lucid firmness, *the murmurs of her-
etic* in flower and leafing Vespignano's rose-lit sky above
Appenine road to Bologna.

Cypress hedges, masses of oleander, magnolia inlaid with
flutter.
"A grey extent of mountain ground tufted irregularly with
ilex and olive."

Refusal of minute and sharp folds: French and German illu-
minated dawns (gowns) and a certain meanness in the
Flemish disposition of drapery.

rubied flower far-away bends
  at intervals
    through framework of each leaf
    sublime form's
    restrained palliate

  low, not desolate/full of sewn
    fields and tended
      pastures Cimabue found him
      drawing sheep
    upon a smooth stone

    "My little drawing to give
    to his Holiness," G.
      took a leaf of vellum with
      brush dipped
    in red and fixing

      arm to side made the limb of
      a pair of compasses
        and turning his hand drew
        a circle so
      perfect it was more

        than enough & thus "Rounder
        than the O of Giotto"
      entered the vernacular  Would a
    circle so produced
      have borne strict witness

to anything other than a draughts-
man's mechanical genius?
"Pennello tinto di rosso"
(brush dipped
in red) misleading in

careless English translation
of *crayon* (lesser made
and rigid) instead of *brush*
hand's appetite
Giotto turned to knowing

---

Papal courtier en route scouting Vatican art among masters
asks Giotto for proofs. ~~Benedict IX~~ (error) Boniface VIII
(correction)

---

opponent rubied flower bend

intervals frame subdued

full found him stone

vellum-red arm

side of turning circle

enough way have witness

to other brush misled

in rigid and lesser drawing


my little vellum red harm

"Dante's indignant expression of the effect of avarice in withering away distinctions of character, and the prophecy of Scrovegno, that his neighbor Vitaliano, when living, should soon be with him, to sit on his left hand, is rendered a little obscure by the transposition of the word 'here'. Cary (the translator, ed. note) has also been afraid of the excessive homeliness of Dante's imagery; 'whiter wing than curd' being in the original 'whiter than butter'. The attachment of the purse to the neck, as a badge of shame, in the Inferno, is found before Dante's time; as, for instance, in the windows of Bourges cathedral (see Plate iii of MM. Martin and Cahier's beautiful work)." John Ruskin

*mostrare un'oca più bianca che burro*

Translator afraid of Dante's butter badge of shame found, for instance, in cathedral (see Plate iii).

Nothing is required for the job but firmness of hand. Nothing more is said and nothing further appears to be thought of expression or invention of devotional sentiment.

Giotto's handmade truth. That a difference might of wrong or right lie in line's thick power shone by accuracy which disdains error.

.

Nothing's sad
nor appears

to be thought
of devotional

sediment. No
thing

required but
firmness

to draw
difference of

wrong or right
in line's thic power

shone by accuracy's
disdaining errorr

## fFretwork

in
fretwork's
stone
 error
even
smallest
incident
suggesting                 error
departure               even

"the languid and degraded condition of becoming merely formal," one sasaid

unexpected starts of effort or flashes of knowledge in accidental directions gradually forming

apprentice to Cimabue, Firenze; footholds, no Byzantine zeroz

Sublime monotony in Constantinople,
magnificent redundance of red and blue          take me
                                                          back

prolonged formality of degraded systems
reminding us of who we were (and we were)

in original noble design. Once sword
and still. Now sword flung head,
flung head. Now still

red hands in white air knit. Slipped parts of
speech retain and invest their knots. evenness.
                                        evidence.

| we were | we were | we | were |
|---------|---------|----|------|
| red hands | white | flung us | parts |

# THE GREAT SYSTEM OF PERFECT COLOR

Blue. Purple. Scarlet deep
with gold [revealed] on [Sinai]
by [GOD] as [noblest]
Others chiefly green
with white & black
used in points of small mass
to relieve blank color

Byzantine flung repetitions

Could we trade length of dress?
Paint unpredicted folds where thigh
opens outward, joints resist
(large blank surfaces)

— four horizontally (lambs,
too) in doorway — noting
nature's tendency
to circle where heat lifts

Gesture of damp gnawing grief

Forgotten twice,
twice refusal of
of ludicrous, cumbrous sheep       grief
sheep leaned as men              gnawing
flocking terminal lines          vertical
Lines, no draperies, broad masses
arm held stiff to pale colors
leaked in vertical bands
Bands continuing,

continuing to

Real faces needed in *the great system of perfect color,*
and different sorts of hair, G. thought

Joachim,

in spite of gold-bordered cape

and halo backdrop returns

empty-handed, marcelled grey hair

(curled rows). Also shepherds' mauve socks

rolled at ankles like us.

White dog jumps up.

No response from Joachim,

eYeSe sidelong.

                              rounder than

                                    0

His own palpate softens theory's sharp folds

seeing lLargE blank surfaces' close-up seeing

... highest strength marked by unconsciousness of its own
means of making no small scorn of best result's exertion,
intent on other than itself caring little for fruits of each toil
(meanwhile "inferior minds intently watching self's process
and valuing product's evidence"), there cannot remain the
smallest doubt that his mind ...


                love of beauty        love of truth
        entirely free        untinged by
        of weakness          severity


        industry constant      workmanship
        without                accurate
        impatience             without formalism


                        — John Ruskin's Giotto


                    _____


                    large blank surfaces


                    _____

The widows of whiter than butter,

I knew none of them

nor curd's buttery purse nor

shame effect.

Sit away, for instance, to the neck.

In 'here' cathedral's obscure badge.

Texts referred to in this work: *Sulla Cappellina degli Scrovegni nell'Arena di Padova*, Sevatico. Padova. 1836. *The Lives of the Artists*, Giorgio Vasari. 1568. (Trans. George Bull. Penguin. New York. 1965. ) *Giotto and his Works in Padua*, John Ruskin. London: George Allen. 1905.

when new time folds up

*understood and scrupulous*

I would have stayed at home as

                                                  rehearsal

if a bystander plated in gold,

                                                     food

understood and scrupulous among

metal bowls, but a doctor goes

to the Gymnasium where scale is

                                                  in key

brick to the heart and air com-

pletely empties itself, without

gender'd regard, thus I tried

my luck as "you", in neutral,

running with you as we talked,

inside the blue grape hyacinth

                                                  represses

where nature reproduces its

mechanical force, *rughetta*

wild in tomb grass,

*a certain uneven panic*


After tomb grass resistance, the occur-

           under us

ence of retinal loss, health sections

every Monday yet many coming into focus

of rue, woe, looking sideways, sidereal

*normalstrasse*, even hearing the gate

bang shut they could not give up where

truck beds beckon, it is such a one in

skirt length, heartbeat crumpled neatly

on white card, leather shoes with-

out pain, your yellow swimsuit dream

           old movie
               dubs

pinned on paper head-to-toe, retinal

crosswords, a certain uneven panic in

the presence of marble force, meat's

possible greed,

*something grey inside of some other grey*

A constant construction on the
building's surrounds, high whine
of electric saw on fake marble
under us, something grey inside
of some other grey when work is                    digested
going, so I barely notice barking
dogs, very well known people next
to lesser known people, small body
praises Indian broideries, runs
for stethoscope sanction, too late
for champagne, lights turned off
rudely as we look, a wall where                     back yards
hangs the triptych typed on a                        sanctum
small card,

So that I would rethink, after

my first resistance to my doctor,      and all
                                        irritation
never sensing her struggle for

authority, no uniform (like a

New York girls-school-refusal),

lest we get personal and I want
                                        a black
her for my friend but she is my         shirt with
                                        a black
 doctor, irregular and random,          hat with a
                                        jacket with
rescuing strict glass cabinets,         black pants

neatly typed histories in metal

linguistic purses, preferring her

old Smith-Corona crumpled in a

heap, good prints on walls, our

waiting-room ease,

*a violated sorted white*

Crumpled uniform heap, they shut

 the gate before it is not over,

dangling places you've never seen

and could be, similar roses cut,

"his smoothness was a cover-up",

still rowing in *Wannsee,* bumping

on *Berlinerstrasse,* big room and

wall, a violated sorted white with

tablecloths, a little messy crash,

his wife's instant flash-bulb/bent

paint evidence, the sea could not

keep it out, could not keep the

various grey waves just at the

window out,

whatever
prestige

back of
his
jacket

*wet grey slabs against the original*

Awakened to car murder noise, will

hit and hit it (siren under hood),

recalcitrant technical murder noise,                 repeated
                                   honk

boys, TV tennis roar and strut,

my snoring love arise now & go from

sleep's time, cement is grinding and

workers are lobbing wet grey slabs          *motorino*

against the original arch, force

covered and uncovered, disappearing

*gelato* box, flavors and steam, Anna

in elegant green linen with nothing

in her hands, no mother uniform or

business card, odd hidden welts but

never believing,

*girlfriend's wheelchair, gathering combs*

Panned wide to shut door, soundtrack

gritty, moved camera slowly, returning

behind
you

tried not to weep while working, denied

all comfort of bread, backward zoom to

youthful self in camp (dream's concen-

tration excrement gone out of control,

skull with your number), wake up,

"Come forward five at a time", a little

speed now, danger over your shoulder, no    *Berlinerstrasse*
scissors

eating scenes, girlfriend's wheelchair,

gathering combs, your original murder

plot withdrawn, *"non così, non così"* (not

like that), in white collar, camera

forward, open,

*to be in normal car murder noise*


Siren's soundtrack embroideries

have not yet focused the question,

"This key to our apartment . . .

because we were separated . . .                    shaved

numbers on our skulls . . . will not              code

be going", (same waltz in 7/8 time),

every cut rose, lights above in

air raid position, streaming, now

through *Berlinerstrasse,* in *Wann-*

*see* I was myself behind a door and

did not have numbers, compelled to

shower on arrival, aroused from TV

sleep, to be yet here in normal

car murder noise, alive,                          daylight cement *no tablecloths, sitting in his car*


Rose lights overhead ("I said this
would happen . . . go to Switzerland
where everyone is laughing"), the
reason for war is money or one                    not like this
other reason in *rapport,* electric
saw cutting *faux* rose marble floor
importance, waiting for a table to
appear, no tablecloths, sitting in
his car, *gelato* Sunday without                  *(non così)*
chairs, establishing radio zone,
clear view from his window, sound
of lover's snore, compressed air,
no *motorino* repairs will pry open
this waking, all pressing,

*if brief, my love (my judge)*


*Cappuccino, spremuta* at the Bar,

as if this were not car murder war

where we are explosion of plastic

massive force on freeway, we from                    value

Palermo, *airportstrasse, autostrada,*

did persist in spite of, wife next

to one's own corpse, decision to

persist, no *kinder* ever, passion
                                                                    nor children
vigilant, this *amore per la vita,* if                        to him

brief, my love (my judge), poured

cement explosion, existing underpass

threatened name's carved stairway

*Falcone* at our wrist, *egalité,*

*ancora, caffè*

*megaphone whose framework holds air*


Deciduous weekday, pantograph map of spring

repeats former leaves and baby speech,

all-new-everything's rebirthed Bar, polished

marble floor, mirror-fronted appliance life,                    up

turquoise fake sky on unpacked chairs, secure                scale

and obsessive megaphone whose framework holds

air, the scaffolding's metal habit, turquoise

netting hooked through to nothing, imagined

life in sirens, regulars wait at Bar door

for opening night, or morning, sleeves wait

too, territorial shadow-pack researches                    *molto*

tables at *Sergio's,* dividing with certain                    *vicino*

justice fresh pizza dough, parceled in air,

slung high . . . and mug beer,

*less sinister the plot on film, "unveiled"*


Raging dragged child in black-and-white,

part of noise up through scaffolding net,

not seen, soft wet day without windows, the

building sighs, being scraped and drilled,

at every shore some poison leaking, white

tennis shorts, less sinister the plot on                     more

film, "unveiled" as if a "neutered thing"

or the absence of no answer, after many

echoing telephone rings, what the others

are doing, one marriage, a baby safely wet

and another yet drying, as if a single day

could affirm our keeping, as if turquoise

chairs and new mirrors might intercede for          contain

what is found,

*and caught in rescuing the authority of her task*


This almost normal marble day delivers an

urgency in passing — *melone, prosciutto* — and

*il dottore* does pronounce "a clean slate",

yet one girl's school refusal, adjusting her

skirt length, replaces glare-free, glassed                    soon

certificates for blow-up's ancient broidery,              and late

herself aside big stars in Pleiades (a.k.a.

Seven Sisters, six visible from *Wannsee,* a

seventh "lost"), she wanted me for her friend,

at one moment seeming to be found, but she,

not recognizing this and caught in rescuing              spending

the authority of her task, returned to her

glass cabinet, regularly, randomly glancing

towards the door,

*a city's constant and hidden remorse*

In the authority of my task, a city's constant

and hidden remorse beneath construction, so that

I would reconsider years of walking *Berliner-*          as

*strasse* inside air raid siren, early and late          skin

gate's nobility, Keiffer bookshelf scaffolding

and bombed-out paint next to Hannah's red hair

headache, migraine gold angel traveling back-

wards, also *Tempelhof* seen from *der Spargel*

spy tower, & new-leafed dome of synagogue in

gold struck flecky light, so barely noticed

barking dogs returning, jumping recent time,

(it's easy), "But every vein cries out" when
                                                         not
new time folds up, in sleep dewy birds never

stop but human song not yet,          singing

Kathleen Fraser
Rome-Berlin-Wannsee-Rome
5/4/92 – 6/9/92
(for Hannah Moekel-Rieke)

# OTHER CHAX BOOKS

# BOOKS BY KATHLEEN FRASER

*Change of Address*, 1966

*In Defiance (of the Rains)*, 1969

*Little Notes to You from Lucas Street*, 1972

*What I Want*, 1974

*Magritte Series*, 1977

*New Shoes*, 1978

*Each Next*, 1980

*Something (even human voices) in the foreground, a lake*, 1984

*boundayr*, 1987

*Notes preceding trust*, 1988

*from a text . . .* , 1993